Landmark
Events in
American
History

The Terrorist Attacks of
September 11, 2001

Dale Anderson

WORLD ALMANAC® LIBRARY

Please visit our web site at: www.worldalmanaclibrary.com
For a free color catalog describing World Almanac® Library's list of high-quality
books and multimedia programs, call 1-800-848-2928 (USA) or 1-800-387-3178
(Canada). World Almanac® Library's fax: (414) 332-3567.

Library of Congress Cataloging-in-Publication Data

Anderson, Dale, 1953-
　　The terrorist attacks of September 11, 2001 / by Dale Anderson.
　　　　p. cm. — (Landmark events in American history)
　　Summary: Describes the causes, events, people, and legacy of the September 11 terrorist
attacks.
　　Includes bibliographical references and index.
　　ISBN 0-8368-5380-6 (lib. bdg.)
　　ISBN 0-8368-5408-X (softcover)
　　1. September 11 Terrorist Attacks, 2001—Juvenile literature.　2. Terrorism—United States—
Juvenile literature.　[1. September 11 Terrorist Attacks, 2001.　2. Terrorism.]　I. Title.
II. Series.
　　HV6432.7.A3843　2003
　　973.931—dc21　　　　　　　　　　　　　　　　　　　　　　　　　2003047986

First published in 2004 by
World Almanac® Library
330 West Olive Street, Suite 100
Milwaukee, WI　53212　USA

Copyright © 2004 by World Almanac® Library.

Produced by Discovery Books
Editor: Sabrina Crewe
Designer and page production: Sabine Beaupré
Photo researcher: Sabrina Crewe
Maps and diagrams: Stefan Chabluk
World Almanac® Library editorial direction: Mark J. Sachner
World Almanac® Library art direction: Tammy Gruenewald
World Almanac® Library production: Beth Meinholz and Jessica Yanke

Photo credits: AP/Wide World Photos: cover, pp. 4, 9, 11, 14, 16, 17, 20, 25, 32, 33, 35,
38, 39, 40, 43; Corbis: pp. 5, 7, 8, 10, 12, 13, 15, 19, 21, 22, 23, 24, 26, 27, 28, 29, 30,
31, 34, 36, 37, 41, 42.

Printed in the United States of America

1 2 3 4 5 6 7 8 9 07 06 05 04 03

Contents

Introduction

A Normal Day

September 11, 2001, dawned bright and clear on the east coast of the United States. It was a Tuesday, and millions of Americans streamed toward their workplaces to start their days.

Sudden Attacks

Suddenly, at 8:48 A.M., the bright morning turned into a nightmare. A passenger jet slammed into one of the two World Trade Center towers in New York City. About fifteen minutes later, another airplane flew straight into the other tower. Then another jet hit the Pentagon in Arlington, Virginia, adjacent to the nation's capital of Washington, D.C. Yet one more plane crashed to the ground in the open country of western Pennsylvania.

The crashes were the work of **terrorists**, and they carried a deadly toll. More than 250 people died on the four **hijacked** planes. Another 2,797 died in the World Trade Center, and 125 were killed at the Pentagon. It was the worst death toll on American soil since the Civil War.

The twin towers of the World Trade Center towered over Manhattan's other buildings before they were destroyed, as shown in this photograph. The World Trade Center was an international business center, and people from more than eighty countries died in the attacks.

The Targeted Buildings

The terrorists attacked buildings that were symbols of American power. The plane that crashed in Pennsylvania was meant to hit the White House, where the president lives and works, or the Capitol building, where Congress meets.

The Pentagon, as headquarters of the Department of Defense, represents U.S. military strength. Built of concrete in the early 1940s, it is the largest office building in the world and covers 29 acres (11.7 hectares). It is called the Pentagon because it has five sides.

The World Trade Center's twin towers housed hundreds of businesses and symbolized American wealth. When they were completed in the early 1970s, they were the tallest buildings in the world—the north tower was 1,368 feet (417 meters) high, and the south tower stood at 1,362 feet (415 m). The World

An aerial view of the Pentagon as a U.S. jet fighter plane flies over it.

Trade Center also comprised four smaller office buildings, a hotel, an open plaza, a large shopping mall, and two subway stations. About 250,000 people passed through the center every day, including the 50,000 who worked there. The center was owned by the Port Authority of New York and New Jersey and leased to businessman Larry Silverstein.

The Background

Growing Anger

The attacks on September 11 shocked most Americans because they did not understand why anyone could hate the United States so much that he or she would kill innocent people. The seeds of that hatred, however, had been planted many years before. Intense anger against the United States had been growing for a long time in the **Middle East**. There were several causes.

The Founding of Israel

One reason was the founding of Israel, home to many of the world's Jews. The Middle East is made up of many Arab countries, and most Arabs are Muslims, followers of the religion of Islam. In the late 1940s, the **United Nations** developed a plan to form two new countries—one for Jews and one for Arabs—in Palestine in the Middle East. Jews considered the region their ancestral land, and they felt they needed a homeland of their own. Arab and other

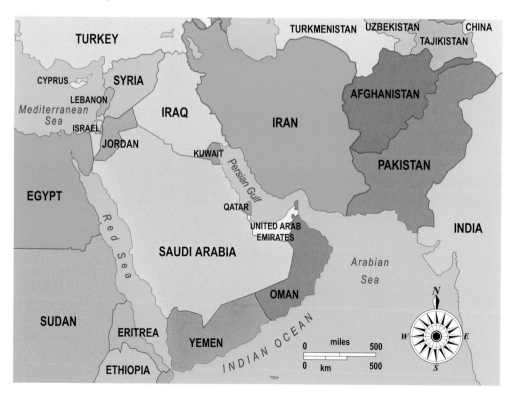

This map shows the countries of the Middle East with Afghanistan and Pakistan (in Asia) to the east and Egypt and Sudan (in Africa) to the west.

Muslim nations opposed the plan because the Palestinian region was also significant to them, and they resented Jews being given land that Arabs had lived on for centuries.

In 1948, the Jewish people nevertheless declared the formation of Israel. Several Arab neighbors attacked the new nation. The United States helped Israel win the conflict.

The Arab-Israeli Conflict

Over the next decades, Israel fought other wars with its Arab

neighbors. In every conflict, the United States backed Israel. The fighting gave Israel control of more land and pushed growing numbers of Palestinians, most of them Muslims, out of their homes. Thousands became **refugees**, forced to flee to other countries.

The West Bank of the Jordan River is a region inhabited by many Palestinians but controlled by Israel. There has been conflict there for many years. This 2002 photo taken on the West Bank shows a young Palestinian throwing a stone at Israeli troops.

Islam and Other Religions

Islam was founded in the 600s by the prophet Muhammad, who lived in what is now Saudi Arabia. Over the centuries, relations between Muslims and Jews and Christians have varied greatly. Jews flourished in Muslim Spain in the 1100s. Many Jews lived in Egypt and other Muslim lands in the 1800s and 1900s. During the Middle Ages, however, Christians launched several wars against Muslims living in Palestine. In these wars, Christians treated their Muslim foes brutally. In the late 1800s, Muslim leaders arose in some parts of Africa and fought Christian armies that had taken control of their countries. Today, Islam has about 1.2 billion followers all over the world.

Over time, some Arab countries made peace with Israel, and many Muslims accepted Israel's right to exist. But Arabs still wanted to see the creation of a new country for the Palestinians. The failure to settle the issue intensified the anger of many Muslims, not only against Jews but against Americans, who gave weapons and money to Israel.

The United States and Iraq

Another reason for Muslim anger against Americans was U.S. actions against the Arab nation of Iraq. In 1990, Iraq invaded its neighbor Kuwait. This move gave control over a large share of the world's supply of oil to Iraq's ruler, the **dictator** Saddam Hussein.

Saddam Hussein (born 1937)

Saddam Hussein began his rise to power in 1968, when the Ba'ath party took control of Iraq's government. In 1979, Saddam became Iraq's leader. The next year, he launched a war against neighboring Iran. The eight-year war cost Iraq tens of thousands of lives and shattered its **economy**. Saddam invaded Kuwait in 1990, hoping to use that nation's oil to rebuild his country. That plan ended with Iraq's defeat in the 1991 Gulf War.

Saddam Hussein at a military parade in the 1990s.

Until 2003, however, Saddam kept his grip on power. His secret police and army eliminated anyone who opposed him. The army even used deadly **chemical weapons** to kill thousands of Iraqis at a time. In March 2003, the United States and Britain invaded Iraq to overthrow Saddam Hussein. Within a month, Saddam's long and cruel regime came to an end.

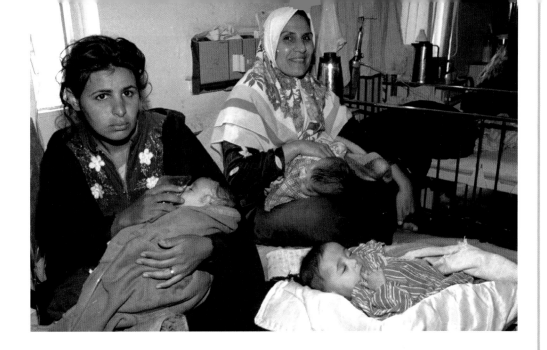

U.S. President George Bush (father of President George W. Bush) led an **alliance** of many nations against Iraq, and in 1991, the allies launched the Gulf War. This military effort succeeded in pushing Iraq's troops out of Kuwait.

U.S. leaders feared that, in revenge, Saddam would use weapons developed in Iraq against Americans. U.S. officials convinced other leaders to stop trade with Iraq until he gave up the weapons.

Since Saddam did not turn over all of Iraq's weapons, the trade **sanctions** remained in effect for many years. As a result, tens of thousands of Iraqis—including children—suffered and died. And because the United States led the movement against Saddam, many Arabs blamed Americans for the suffering of Iraq's people.

Americans in Saudi Arabia

The Gulf War led to yet another cause for Muslim hatred. During and after the war, the United States placed troops in Saudi Arabia,

Result of the Sanctions

"The *British Journal of Independence Studies* placed the number of Iraqis who had died as a result of the sanctions at 1.5 million, half of whom were under five years old. . . . These statistics are the direct results of the outside siege imposed by America and Britain."

Said Aburish, writer, 2000

Hostages at the U.S. embassy in Iran are led outside, blindfolded, on the day of their capture in November 1979. They were kept for more than a year before they were released.

which borders Iraq and is home to several of Islam's holiest places. Some Muslims believed that the presence of U.S. troops—many of them Christians—on this holy soil was an outrage.

U.S. Support of Dictators

Despite its support of Israel, the United States depended heavily on some Arab nations' large supplies of oil. Many of these countries were led by monarchs who handed power from one generation to another or by dictators who allowed their people few freedoms. Many poor or oppressed Arabs resented the fact that the U.S. government supported these harsh rulers primarily to satisfy the United States' need for Arab oil.

The Rise of Terrorism

Resentment about all these issues built for years. Starting in the late 1960s, a few **extremists** began to launch terrorist attacks against the people of the countries they hated. The first attacks struck Israelis, but in 1979, more than 50 Americans were taken **hostage** in Iran and held in captivity for more than a year. In 1983, terrorists in Lebanon exploded a bomb at the U.S. embassy, killing 63 people, and then bombed a U.S. military barracks, killing more than 240 Marines.

In 1985, Americans on a passenger jet and on a cruise ship were taken as hostages. Each time, the terrorists killed an American they held captive. Three years later, terrorists blew a passenger jet out of the sky by hiding bombs in luggage that went on board. The blast killed 259 people on the plane, most of them Americans.

Attacks on American Soil

In the 1990s, terrorists struck within the United States. In 1993, Muslim extremists packed explosives into a vehicle and parked it in a garage under one of the World Trade Center towers. The blast killed six people and wounded hundreds more.

By the late 1990s, many Americans thought that the danger of terrorism had passed. But a secret organization—called al Qaeda—had formed and was growing stronger. Its leaders were planning fresh assaults on the United States.

The World Trade Center was first attacked by terrorists on February 26, 1993. This photograph taken the next day shows the hole made by the bomb that exploded in the underground garage.

Chapter 2

Network of Terror

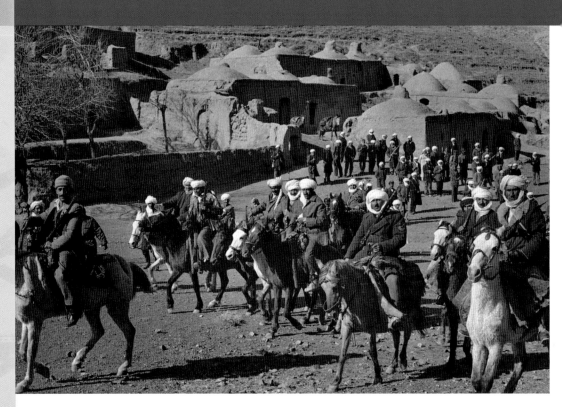

A group of *mujahadeen* rebel forces set out on horseback in a raid against Soviet positions in Afghanistan in January 1980. The *mujahadeen* believed they were fighting a holy war for Islam.

Orphans of the War

"They were literally the orphans of the war, the rootless and the restless, the jobless and the economically deprived. . . . Their simple belief in a [pure] Islam which had been drummed into them by simple village [teachers] was the only prop they could hold on to and which gave their lives some meaning."

Ahmed Rashid, author, 2000, describing those who became rebels in Afghanistan

Afghanistan's Muslim Rebels

In the late 1970s, a group of **socialists** took control of the government in Afghanistan, a mostly Muslim nation in Asia that neighbors Iran. Soon after, Muslim rebels began to fight the newly formed government. Afghanistan's large and powerful neighbor, the Soviet Union, then sent troops to help the socialist government fight the rebels.

The rebels, who received help from the United States, were called *mujahadeen*, which means "those who fight *jihad*." *Jihad*, in Arabic, means the struggle by Muslims to please God. This can be done by being virtuous or by helping others, but the term is also applied to the struggle against "enemies of Islam."

The fight against the non-Muslim Soviets attracted many Muslims, not just Afghanis. In the late 1980s, Soviet leaders gave up and pulled out their troops.

The Taliban Emerge

A civil war then broke out as different sides struggled to become the leading power in Afghanistan. Finally, in the late 1990s, a group called the Taliban took control of most of the country. The Taliban had been one of the *mujahadeen* groups supported with money and weapons by the United States, but many nations soon refused to have relations with this new government. This was because of their harsh leadership and also because they gave a home to Muslim extremists, such as Osama bin Laden.

Muslim Extremists

The war against the Soviet Union had turned many Muslims into tough, experienced fighters. It also helped spread extreme religious ideas. Osama bin Laden, who came to Afghanistan to fight the Soviet Union, emerged as a leader among

The Taliban

Taliban is a Persian word meaning "students," and the people who formed the group devoutly studied and believed in Islam. They disliked the growing influence of American culture—clothes, food, music, and movies—in the Muslim world. Once in power, the Taliban created harsh laws based on strict Islamic teachings. They banned entertainment and forced women and girls to stay in their homes. The Taliban harshly punished and even executed people who broke those laws.

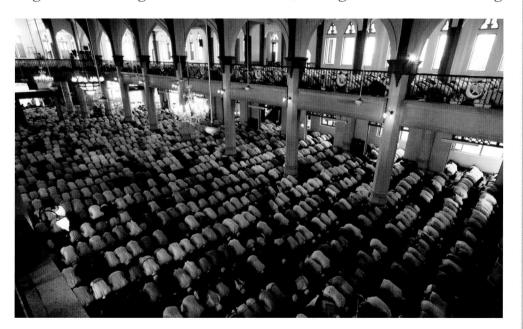

Prayer is one of the five pillars of Islam, and devout Muslims worship five times a day. The other four pillars of Islam are faith, alms-giving (or charity), fasting, and pilgrimage to holy places.

13

these extremists. He used his large personal fortune to help finance *mujahadeen* and set up camps for them.

When the war with the Soviet Union ended, the *mujahadeen* looked for a new cause. Bin Laden formed an organization that came to be called al Qaeda ("*al-Qa'ida*" is Arabic for "the base"). This group was dedicated to fighting against Israel and the United States. After Saudi Arabia allowed U.S. troops on holy soil, bin Laden added the Saudi government to his list of enemies.

Forming a Network

Bin Laden began to gather his forces in Sudan, in Africa, while agents around the world recruited young Muslims to join the cause. Bin Laden formed several camps where these recruits learned how to fight and carry out terrorist attacks.

When the Taliban took control of Afghanistan, bin Laden and al Qaeda made the country their base. They set up many camps and continued to train recruits. Al Qaeda experimented with chemical weapons and tried to obtain materials used to make devastating nuclear bombs. Bin Laden's fortune helped pay for this effort, as did money from a huge network that sold illegal drugs.

A large part of the worldwide illegal drug trade starts in the poppy fields of Afghanistan, where poor farmers survive by growing the opium poppies that are used to make heroin. It ends in the sale of illegal drugs to addicts, and huge sums of money from this trade are funneled into terrorism.

Osama bin Laden (born 1957)

Nothing in Osama bin Laden's early life signaled that he would become one of the world's most feared men. He was born in Saudi Arabia, the son of a rich Yemeni family, and inherited millions of dollars when his father died in 1968.

In his teens, bin Laden grew more religious. His Muslim beliefs intensified while he was in college, where he was influenced by **radical** teachers. Bin Laden came to believe that Muslims had to launch a *jihad* against western culture. Bin Laden graduated from college in 1981. During the fighting in Afghanistan, he met other extremist thinkers who were calling for a war against Christians. Bin Laden gave up the comfortable life of a rich man to join this war, and he became a leader among radical Muslims.

Preaching *Jihad*

Bin Laden harbored deep hatred against the United States. According to a Saudi who knew him, even in the 1980s, bin Laden was saying, "The next battle is going to be with America." In 1996, he issued a declaration against the United States. The chilling statement called on Muslims throughout the world to kill Americans and Israelis.

This aerial photo shows a terrorist training camp in Afghanistan that was targeted by U.S. missiles in August 1998. The attacks were in response to terrorist bombings of U.S. embassies in Kenya and Tanzania.

In 1998, bin Laden formed an alliance between al Qaeda and other radical Muslim groups. They claimed that Americans were killing Muslim **civilians**, and this was their justification for killing U.S. civilians. They urged Muslims to kill Americans "anywhere, anytime, and wherever possible."

Al Qaeda Attacks

Also in 1998, al Qaeda made its first attack on the United States. In a carefully planned operation, terrorists drove truck bombs up to the U.S. embassies in two cities in Africa. The bombs ripped through the buildings and killed more than 220 people. Twelve were Americans, but most of the victims were Africans.

The U.S. government declared that bin Laden was responsible for the attack. The U.S. Navy launched powerful cruise missiles against al Qaeda bases in Afghanistan. Although the attacks damaged the camps, they did little to hurt the organization.

On December 14, 1999, Ahamed Ressam, a man trained in al Qaeda's camps, was arrested as he tried to enter the United States. His car was full of explosives, which he planned to use to blow up the busy international Los Angeles airport.

In 2000, al Qaeda struck again, in Yemen in the Middle East. As a U.S. Navy ship, the USS *Cole*, sat in a harbor, a small boat loaded with explosives was blown up near the ship. The blast ripped a huge hole in the ship's side, killing seventeen American sailors.

Meanwhile, men trained by al Qaeda spread throughout the world. By 2001, officials believed the terrorists could be found in more than forty countries. Some of them were working toward the September 11 attacks.

On October 12, 2000, a terrorist bomb exploded next to this U.S. Navy destroyer, the USS *Cole*. It was al Qaeda's last attack on an American target before the September 11 attacks.

The Attacks

The Plan

The plan for the September 11 attacks called for four teams of hijackers to take control of four passenger jets and fly the airplanes into important American buildings. The impact of the crash would ignite the jet fuel, turning the planes into devastating bombs. After the attacks, Osama bin Laden was quoted as saying that the terrorists did not expect the attacks to destroy the buildings. They hoped, at most, to damage them badly.

The planners chose airplanes making long-distance flights. These planes carried more fuel and would make a bigger explosion.

Getting Ready

Planners had to find enough men willing to go to certain death. One al Qaeda leader later said this part was not hard. "We had a large surplus of brothers willing to die as **martyrs**," he said. Some team members needed training to fly jets, and that would take time.

The attacking planes all took off between 7:59 and 8:20 A.M. Eastern Daylight Time on September 11, 2001. By 9:00 A.M., three of the four were in control of the hijackers and heading for their targets.

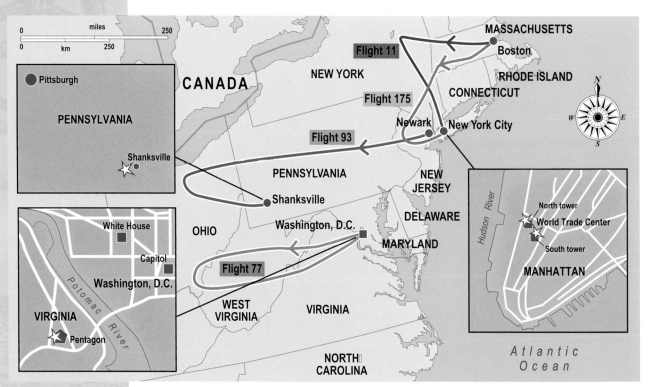

Meanwhile, the four teams had to gather in the United States and develop their plan. When the attacks were finally made, they would have to be well coordinated. The four hijackings would take place around the same time to prevent officials from doing anything to stop any of the airplanes. And each group would need to gain control of the cockpit so their own pilot could fly the plane.

The terrorists ran into few problems as their plan progressed. By late August 2001, the teams were in place.

A video camera at the airport in Portland, Maine, taped terrorist Mohammed Atta (right) as he passed through security on his way to Boston early on September 11. Atta was the leader of the hijackers on that day.

The Hijackers

Nineteen men carried out the September 11 attacks. Thirteen of them—twelve from Saudi Arabia—were included simply to help gain control of the airplanes. Two, both Saudis about twenty-five years old, helped coordinate the movements of the teams.

Four were the pilots who flew the planes after they were seized. Hani Hanjour was a twenty-nine-year-old Saudi who had been in the United States since 1996. Ziad Jarrah was a twenty-six-year-old from Lebanon. Marwan al-Shehhi, from the United Arab Emirates, was only twenty-three years old. While living in Germany, he became friends with Mohammed Atta, the fourth pilot and the main architect of the attacks. Atta, at thirty-three the oldest of the nineteen men, was an Egyptian. Atta and al-Shehhi apparently both traveled to Afghanistan in 1999 and trained at an al Qaeda camp there. During that time, Atta met Osama bin Laden and discussed the idea of using hijacked airplanes to attack American buildings.

The North Tower

The first hijacking was of American Airlines Flight 11. Soon after the plane took off from Boston, Mohammed Atta and four companions seized control. Near Albany, New York, Atta changed the plane's course to head south for New York City. About half an hour later, it smashed into the north tower of the World Trade Center.

The airplane knifed into the building between the 95th and 103rd floors. Adam Mayblum, who worked in the north tower, remembered what it was like: "The building lurched violently and shook as if it were an earthquake. . . . The building seemed to move 10 to 20 feet (3 to 6 m) in each direction." Fires broke out everywhere as highly flammable jet fuel spewed out of the plane's wings and burst into flames. Many of the building's elevators stopped working.

People in the building began to escape by taking stairways that were still usable. Some people did not leave but waited for instructions from emergency workers. Others—on the floors above the crash—had no choice but to wait. All the stairways and elevators to the very top of the building had been destroyed.

Above the ninety-fifth floor, smoke pours from the World Trade Center's north tower shortly after it was hit. People trying to escape from the upper floors found there was no way out.

U.S. President George W. Bush listens as White House Chief of Staff Andrew Card informs him of the terrorist attacks. The president was visiting an elementary school classroom in Sarasota, Florida, when he received the news.

A Second Attack

When the first airplane struck the north tower, many people began to leave the south tower as well. A few minutes later, officials declared that the second building was safe and that workers could return to work.

At this point, it was still not clear what was happening. Even people who knew that a plane had crashed into the north tower believed

The September 11 Attacks

Flight	From–To	Target	Passengers and Crew	Hijackers	Time of Crash
American 11	Boston–Los Angeles	World Trade Center north tower	92	5	8:48 A.M.
United 175	Boston–Los Angeles	World Trade Center south tower	65	5	9:03 A.M.
American 77	Washington–Los Angeles	Pentagon	64	5	9:37 A.M.
United 93	Newark–San Francisco	White House or Capitol building	44	4	10:10 A.M.

This series of photographs shows the second attack, as the hijacked airplane approaches and then hits the World Trade Center's south tower (on the left in each picture). A huge hole can be seen in the north tower (on the right in each picture) where it was hit by the first plane minutes earlier.

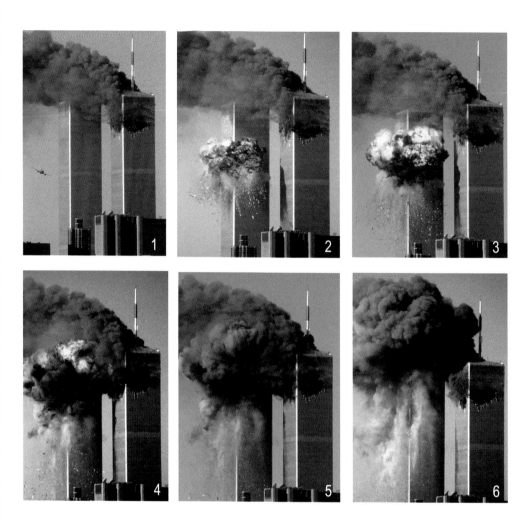

that it was simply a horrible accident. Fifteen minutes after the first crash, however, the second hijacked jet slammed into the other tower.

The South Tower

News cameras, already showing the results of the first crash, were there to record the second airplane smashing into the south tower. ABC newsman Charles Gibson said, "This looks like it is some sort of concerted effort to attack the World Trade Center."

The Burning Towers

"I could not believe what I was seeing—both buildings were on fire with flames shooting out of them about a hundred feet high. Huge plumes of thick black smoke were billowing out of them and when I looked at [the south tower] you could still see the tail end of the jet hanging out of the building."

Eric Levine, who worked in the south tower

The second plane hit its target on an angle, tearing into even more floors than the first. Frightened people crowded onto stairways and any working elevators to escape. Meanwhile, fires raged from the huge hole made by the plane. Debris—pieces of the building, shattered airplane parts, and office equipment—flew to the ground. Dust and ashes began to cover everything.

A Third Attack

News of the attacks spread across the country, and many Americans watched the burning towers on their televisions. Tom Seibert was one. He was at work in his office at the Pentagon. "You know, the next best target would be us," Seibert said to his companions. Just five minutes later, the third hijacked airplane plowed into the building.

The Pentagon is a huge office building, home to thousands of workers. The force of the plane tore a gaping hole in one of the building's five sides. The hole reached from the ground to the roof, five stories up, and back into the five rings of rooms and corridors that make up the building. Soon soldiers, office workers, firefighters, and others were doing what they could to find and rescue people. Firefighters also tried to put out the flames. They had to work many hours—late that night, the fire was still burning.

This photo shows how the crash and subsequent fire damaged the huge Pentagon complex. This picture was taken three days later, when firefighters and rescue workers were still looking for victims in the rubble.

A Tower of Rubble

Meanwhile, hundreds of New York City police, firefighters, and other rescue personnel arrived at the World Trade Center. Firefighters streamed up the stairways of the north tower and the south tower. They reassured the people coming down. They helped the people who needed it. They tried to reach—and save—the people on the upper floors.

Taking Action

Once they realized that the hijackings were underway, Air Force officers ordered fighter planes into the sky. They were ordered to find the two airplanes heading for New York. They could not arrive in time to stop the planes from crashing into the towers, however.

Just minutes after the second tower was hit, the federal government

Grounded planes sit at an airport in New Jersey on September 12, while smoke and dust pour from the World Trade Center site in Manhattan.

closed the airports in the New York area. At 9:30 A.M., radar showed an unidentified plane—American Flight 77—heading toward Washington, D.C. and Arlington, Virginia. Air Force officers ordered fighter jets into the air to intercept it. They also arrived too late.

A few minutes later, the federal government ordered every airplane over the United States to land at the nearest airport. For the first time in history, all air traffic over the country was stopped. Officials also ordered everyone to leave the White House and the Capitol building, where Congress meets. Then, officials began tracking the fourth hijacked plane, United Flight 93. Fighter pilots were told to destroy the airplane, if necessary, to stop it from hitting a target. Before they could reach it, the plane crashed in western Pennsylvania.

As the south tower came tumbling down, people fled from danger. The twin towers were so huge that when they fell, they damaged buildings and streets all around them.

But the twin towers were becoming more and more dangerous. The planes had damaged the strong central cores that held the buildings in place. They had also blown away many of the steel columns on the outside that helped support the structure. That meant that the remaining columns had an even heavier load to bear. And the fires that raged in the towers neared 1,000° F (538° C), a temperature that can soften steel.

The Towers Collapse

At 9:59 A.M., less than an hour after it was hit, the south tower began to collapse. It only took about fifteen seconds for the entire building to come down. Firefighter Marcel Claes was in the north tower at the time and heard the other one go down. He said the noise was "as if a tractor-trailer was rolling through your living room."

The north tower, although the first to be hit, was the second to fall. This series of photos captured its collapse.

People outside the south tower were blinded by the thick smoke and had difficulty breathing in the dusty air. Falling debris from the tower destroyed another building to the east.

In the north tower, people continued to stream out. Rescue workers realized that they, too, had to leave and began to evacuate. Then, at 10:28, the north tower also came tumbling down.

"Let's Roll"

At around the same time, another drama was playing out on the fourth hijacked airplane, United Flight 93. As the hijackers turned

A Giant Roar

"There was a distant, yet giant crumbling sound. That sound became a giant roar. . . . We saw the upper floors of [the south tower] give way, and break away from the rest of the tower. Then, almost in slow motion, the building fell straight down.

"Through the haze and smoke, I could see the silhouette of the building as it . . . fell straight down. Finally, there was nothing left of the south tower but a thin spine of elevator shafts. And then that seemed to disintegrate."

Brendan MacWade, who watched the collapse after escaping from the north tower

it to head for Washington, D.C., passengers made phone calls to their families. From these calls, some learned of the attacks on the World Trade Center and the Pentagon.

As the minutes ticked away and the airplane sped toward the nation's capital, the passengers discussed what to do. Passenger Tom Burnett called his wife and told her that they had decided to try to retake the airplane. "If they're going to drive this plane into the ground then we've got to do something," he said. Todd Beamer, unable to reach his wife, spoke with a woman who worked for the phone company. He asked her to contact his family and then prayed with her. The worker then heard Beamer say, "Are you guys ready? Let's roll."

Soon after, the airplane's cockpit tape recorder captured sounds of a struggle. There were angry words and screams, and the plane zigzagged. Minutes later, it crashed into an open field near Shanksville, Pennsylvania. All people on board died in the fiery crash. The passengers and crew had stopped the terrorists from hitting another building.

The People Who Died
All 232 passengers and 33 crew members of the four airplanes died in the crashes. At the World Trade Center, about 2,800 people died

Emergency workers examine the site where United Flight 93 crashed near Shanksville, Pennsylvania. Nobody on board survived the crash, but the passengers and crew who resisted the hijackers had helped prevent further deaths on the ground.

A view of the World Trade Center site on September 15, 2001, shows how a large area of lower Manhattan was damaged by the attacks.

because of the attacks. More than 6,000 were wounded. New Yorkers mourned the loss of 343 firefighters, several police officers, and other rescue workers who had given their lives to save others.

At the Pentagon, 125 people were killed and 88 more were injured. A stroke of good luck kept the Pentagon death toll down: the area hit by the plane had recently been renovated and many workers had not yet moved back into their offices.

Scenes of Horror at the World Trade Center

The destruction of the twin towers brought terrible, unforgettable sights. Louis Garcia, a medic, saw people who had died "burned from head to toe." Many people on the uppermost floors jumped from the buildings, choosing to fall ninety or more floors rather than face being burned alive. In some cases, people took hold of each other's hands before they jumped. The sight was seared into the memories of those who witnessed it.

Chuck Allen, who worked on the eighty-third floor of the north tower, survived the impact of the attack and made it out before the tower fell. When he reached the plaza outside the tower, Allen saw the bodies—sometimes only parts of bodies—of airplane passengers. They still had seatbelts wrapped around them.

The Survivors

New York City Mayor Rudolph Giuliani talked to reporters on the afternoon of September 11. When asked about the possible losses, he gave a gloomy prediction. "More than any of us can bear," he said. All day long—and for many weeks afterward—the fear was that the losses would be staggering. Tens of thousands of people worked in the twin towers, and thousands more visited each day as tourists. The Pentagon employed twenty thousand workers.

Although the death toll was high, it could have been much worse. The planes struck early in the day, and some people had not arrived at work. The vast majority of people who were there were able to escape. Some got out on their own; others were helped by strangers. Yet others survived because of the work of rescuers.

In one lucky twist, a group of New York firefighters survived because they had been rescuing someone else. They were helping an elderly woman down a stairwell when the north tower collapsed. She moved slowly—too slowly, they feared at the time. But by chance, the very section of the stairway where they were remained standing when the building collapsed. In the afternoon, the woman and nine firefighters were rescued.

Grief and Loss

Many of the survivors had scars. Some were physical, but the deeper scars were emotional. That was the pain felt by firefighters who survived when their friends did not, or by people whose husbands, wives, parents, or children died in the attacks.

On Friday, September 14, the country took a moment to grieve for the dead. Synagogues, mosques, and churches across the country held services. People used religious readings and prayers to try to find comfort in their sadness and fear.

Thousands of people in the twin towers survived the attacks on September 11. Many were rescued by the efforts of firefighters, who then lost their own lives as the buildings came down.

Chapter 4

The Impact at Home

Rescue workers at the scene of the destroyed World Trade Center towers continued to comb the site for survivors long after hope began to fade. The overwhelming scale of the task did not diminish their efforts.

A Lot of Hard Days

"There were a lot of hard days and we considered good days [to be those] days when we found remains, [because] there was a day we could send something back to a family that was always waiting for that phone call."

Ed Benanati, who worked on the World Trade Center cleanup, 2002

Search and Rescue

After the buildings collapsed, workers poured over the site of the fallen twin towers. At first, they hoped desperately to rescue people who might miraculously have survived the collapse. After the second day, however, not a single survivor was dug out.

Gradually, then, hope faded. The work continued, but it was a grimmer task—recovering the remains of the dead so they could be properly buried. New York's firefighters were dedicated to the search for their comrades. Each time one was found, all work would stop and the body would be carried out past a line of grieving workers.

Cleaning Up

Another task also began—cleaning up the World Trade Center. It took more than eight months to clear away more than 1.6 million tons of debris. The debris came not only from the twin towers, but from nearby buildings that had been destroyed by their collapse.

Cleanup crews used powerful machines to lift out the heavy pieces of steel and concrete that could not be taken out by hand. They had to work carefully to avoid damaging any bodies lying in the rubble. And investigators had to sift through everything that was uncovered to find evidence about the attacks and the attackers.

Rudolph Giuliani (born 1944)

Rudolph Giuliani was born in Brooklyn, a borough of New York City. He went to school, college, and law school in the city. As a prosecuting attorney, he earned a reputation for being tough on crime. Giuliani was elected mayor of New York in 1993. He continued his firm line, leading a strong police effort to halt the rising rate of crime in the city. The effort worked,

Mayor Rudolph Giuliani (right) at the World Trade Center site with United Nations Secretary-General Kofi Annan (center) and New York Governor George Pataki (left) on September 18, 2001.

and crime dropped throughout the 1990s. This success helped Giuliani win re-election in 1997, but his toughness had aspects that were not popular. Critics thought that he did not have enough concern for prisoners' rights. And relations between New York's police and the black community were poor throughout his time in office. After September 11, much of that was forgotten as Giuliani's strong leadership showed New Yorkers that, although the city had taken an awful blow, it would survive. Guiliani's term as mayor ended in 2002.

Rebuilding

The Pentagon did not suffer as much as the New York City site. Only one part of the building had been damaged, and the number of victims was much smaller. Still, many thousands of square feet of the Pentagon had to be rebuilt.

Planners aimed to have the Pentagon repairs completed by the first anniversary of the crash. People worked around the clock for more than 270 days and nights, finishing the work ahead of schedule. Workers were so dedicated to their task that they were angry when bosses told them to take holidays off.

Honoring Heroes

In Pennsylvania, the citizens of Shanksville quietly made a memorial to honor the passengers of United Flight 93, who had fought the hijackers of the fourth airplane. Hundreds of people visited each day. Many left behind photographs, messages, wreaths, or flowers to show their gratitude for what the passengers and crew had done.

A year after the attacks in September 2001, the memorial near Shanksville still attracted visitors who wanted to honor the bravery of the passengers and crew on United Flight 93.

In every state, there is a National Guard, a force of part-time soldiers trained and ready to respond to national and state emergencies. After the September 11 attacks, National Guard members were posted at airports around the country to help safeguard against further terrorist attacks.

Helping Victims and Their Families

While the cleanup and the rebuilding went on, people across the country wanted to do something to help. Many went immediately after the attacks to Red Cross centers, where they donated blood for victims. Others gave clothing and food, and people farther away

The Human Impact

As the attacks were first reported, people focused on the numbers of victims. Soon, however, names, faces, and personal stories emerged from the statistics and the rubble. New web sites appeared, telling victims' and survivors' stories. *The New York Times* ran a series that lasted many months, honoring those who died in the World Trade Center attacks. Each story revealed the background, the hopes, and the dreams of ordinary people whose lives had been snuffed out. Other stories emerged that brought home what the deaths meant to victims' families. For them, the pain continued. Aimee Dechavez spoke for many when she visited the twin towers site in 2002. "They never found any part of my brother," she said, "so for us he is here. It is the last place he was seen." One policemen told other visitors to the site how workers heard cell phones still ringing hopefully inside bodybags as they brought out the dead—calls that would never be answered.

helped by donating money. Charities raised hundreds of millions of dollars to be used to help the families. They also helped survivors who had lost their jobs or businesses.

Looking for the Terrorists

The U.S. government moved quickly to identify the people who carried out the attacks. Before September 11 was over, the government named al Qaeda as the chief suspect. Al Qaeda did not take credit for the attack at first, but videotape of Osama bin Laden surfaced early in the following year. It

These prisoners were members of al Qaeda or the Taliban, captured by the U.S. military in Afghanistan in late 2001. They and other terrorist suspects were held at the U.S. military base at Guantanamo Bay on the island of Cuba.

Preventing Another Attack

For the first weeks after the attacks, air force jet fighters patrolled the skies above the nation's largest cities. The nation's passenger airplanes were kept on the ground for two days, and the airport nearest to Washington, D.C., was kept closed for many weeks. Security at all airports was tightened as National Guard troops were sent to many airports. Later, Congress passed a law that put the workers who handled air-port security under the control of the federal government. The law also required airports to install machines that could x-ray all luggage to look for bombs. The government began hiring more armed air marshals and putting them on many flights. Steps were taken to tighten security around nuclear power plants and other key danger spots.

was clear from his comments that he had known about the attacks in advance.

The U.S. government did not wait for these tapes to be convinced that bin Laden was responsible. It began a search for him and several other al Qaeda leaders. With the help of officials in other countries, the president also launched an attempt to cut off al Qaeda's money supply. Meanwhile, police and Federal Bureau of Investigation (FBI) agents began to pick up hundreds of Muslims living in the United States.

Troubling Issues

Americans favored many of the steps the government had taken to improve security. Some people, however, worried that the government might go too far. They complained that holding Muslim immigrants and visitors without charging them with a crime was unfair. They said that some Muslim Americans were being denied their full rights. The debate over this issue continued for many months.

In 2001, more than 5 million U.S. citizens were Muslims, and they were as horrified by the terrorist attacks as everyone else. These two young Muslim Americans attended a peace rally organized by the Muslim community in Dallas, Texas, in October 2001.

Chapter 5

The War on Terror

All over the world, **moderate** Muslims spoke out against terrorism and extremist violence after September 11. At the U.S. embassy in Kuwait, people lay flowers and messages in memory of the victims.

Support from Around the World

The September 11 attacks shocked people all over the world. Ordinary people expressed their sympathy for the victims of the attacks. Some cautioned Americans to be mindful of how their government's policies had hurt others, and many more feared war.

Russia's Vladimir Putin was the first leader to contact President George W. Bush with words of sympathy and a pledge of support in the fight against terrorism. Other nations quickly followed. One of the strongest voices was that of British Prime Minister Tony Blair,

Words of Support

"I am Muslim. My eyes got wet when I saw . . . just before [the south tower] collapsed, . . . people waving shirts in their hands for help. I was just praying if some helicopters come and would rescue them—but they never got that chance. . . . God, how cruel it is to kill innocent people. It is the same red blood, which ran in all humans."

Nadeem Malik of Belgium, reacting to television images of the September 11 attacks

who said, "This is not a battle between the United States and terrorism, but between the free and **democratic** world and terrorism."

A Warning to Terrorists

Within days of September 11, Bush and other top government officials had decided to use the attacks to rally the world in a fight

The Leaders

Leading the nation's response to the attacks was President George W. Bush (born 1946). In 2000, Bush became president in one of the closest elections ever. In his public speeches after September 11, Bush expressed grief for the dead and sympathy for their families. He spoke of his pride for the professional rescuers and volunteers who had rallied to help. He vowed to seek out the guilty.

Colin Powell (left), George W. Bush (center), and Donald Rumsfeld (right) at a White House cabinet meeting in November 2001.

Working closely with Bush was Secretary of State Colin Powell (born 1937). Powell was greatly respected around the world. He had joined the army after college and served for many years. Powell played an important role in the victory against Iraq in the Gulf War and had risen higher in the military than any African American before him. In the early 1990s, Powell retired from the military, but he came back to Washington in 2001 to become secretary of state.

Donald Rumsfeld (born 1932), secretary of defense, was another close Bush advisor. He was also a veteran of Washington and had run the Defense Department in the 1970s. He was known for his blunt way of speaking and his strong leadership of the country's armed forces.

against terrorism. On September 20, the president demanded that the Taliban leaders of Afghanistan turn over all al Qaeda activists in their country. If they did not, he warned, the Taliban would suffer the same fate as al Qaeda.

War

The Taliban refused to hand bin Laden over, and the U.S. government gained some international support for military action. On October 7, 2001, U.S. and British forces (called the "allied forces") began bombing Taliban targets in Afghanistan. Special forces of highly trained fighters were sent into the country. Some worked with Afghan rebels who had been fighting the Taliban for years and had united into a group called the Northern Alliance. After just two months of fighting, the Taliban hold on Afghanistan collapsed.

Afghanis set up a temporary government in late 2001. That government faced many challenges. The country was poor, and years of war had destroyed roads, bridges, and cities. The different groups that had fought against the Taliban did not always

The U.S. attacks on Afghanistan were successful in destroying the Taliban's defenses and bringing down its government. In this picture, a Northern Alliance fighter who supported the U.S. invasion stands by the wreckage of Taliban radar equipment.

In January 2002, U.S. Navy SEALs explore a cave that had been used for terrorist operations in eastern Afghanistan. It was originally thought that Osama bin Laden was hiding in Afghanistan's network of caves.

agree with each other. It would take a long time to overcome years of mistrust and anger and to rebuild the broken country.

An Elusive Enemy

During the fighting against the Taliban, the Northern Alliance and allied forces moved into many areas that al Qaeda had occupied. They seized vast amounts of weapons and destroyed the camps that had been al Qaeda training centers for thousand of young men. Early in December 2001, U.S. and Northern Alliance forces surrounded an important al Qaeda hideout in Afghanistan's mountains. It was thought that Osama bin Laden himself may be inside.

After days of intense bombing, the allied forces moved into the caves where al Qaeda fighters had been hiding. Along with weapons, they discovered computer files, paper records, and other evidence that told much about al Qaeda. But whatever fighters had been there had disappeared. Early in 2002, there were other battles between allied forces and al Qaeda fighters. Although the allied troops were victorious, they did not find Osama bin Laden.

A Continued Threat

Over time, a few top al Qaeda officials were caught. The head of al Qaeda's military forces was killed in late 2001. Abu Zubaydah, one of the group's top planners, was captured in April 2002. Ramzi Binalshibh, who helped plan the attacks, was arrested in September 2002. On March 1, 2003, Khalid Shaikh Mohammed, suspected to be the mastermind behind the September 11 attacks, was arrested. Hundreds of other suspects were picked up in many countries.

Many terrorists remained at large, however, and attacks continued. Late in 2002, bombs ripped through a nightclub on the island of Bali, in Indonesia. More than two hundred people died in the blast, and many more were hurt. This time, the main targets were not Americans but Australians on vacation in Bali. Investigators were certain it was the work of al Qaeda. Soon after, another set of attacks targeted Israelis. It was clear that al Qaeda still remained a threat to the world.

Showdown in Iraq

While the effort to track down al Qaeda continued, another storm was brewing. During 2002, the U.S. government charged that not only did Iraq house highly destructive weapons, but that Iraqi leader Saddam Hussein had connections with al Qaeda and might

In December 2002, weapons inspectors were sent by the United Nations to look for weapons in Iraq. This inspector is examining containers in a chemical plant to see if there is any evidence of the manufacture of weapons.

provide the terrorists with weapons. In December 2002, as United Nations inspectors entered Iraq to look for evidence of weapons, the United States began preparations to attack the country.

Invasion

The UN inspectors found little, but they questioned Iraq's cooperation. Should military action be taken? The debate about the rights and wrongs of an invasion raged around the world in a way that had never happened before. In spite of protests at home and abroad, the United States and Britain entered Iraq on March 21, 2003, declaring their intention to disarm Iraq, remove Saddam Hussein from power, and create a fair government in Iraq.

In just a few weeks, with little Iraqi resistance in the face of overwhelming military power, Iraq fell to U.S. and British troops. Even the the capital of Baghdad succumbed quickly after heavy bombing destroyed royal palaces, military headquarters, and the key positions of Saddam's army.

In April 2003, after the collapse of Saddam Hussein's regime, thousands of Iraqis headed back to Baghdad. They had fled their homes during the U.S. bombing campaign.

41

Conclusion

Rallying the Country

The September 11 attacks united most Americans. There was a surge of **patriotism** after the attacks as people rallied to show love for their nation. More honor was given to people serving in the armed forces. There was renewed respect for police and firefighters, who put their lives on the line for others.

The United States in the World

At the same time, however, Americans were examining their attitudes to other nations. People in other countries worried that the September 11 attacks would not change those attitudes. Many encouraged the United States to take a more active role in settling the Israeli-Palestinian conflict. Muslims, while they condemned the killing of innocent people in the attacks, still complained about U.S. policy in the Middle East. They warned that, if nothing changed, more and more bitter people would appear—people so angry at the United States that they would be willing to kill Americans if they got the chance.

In the Middle East, conflict continued with a series of suicide bombings by the Palestinians, as Arabs and Israelis continued to clash over territory and other issues. A suicide bomb killed at least ten Israelis on this bus in April 2002.

U.S. flags were everywhere after September 11. In this parade on Thanksgiving Day 2001, police and other rescue workers carried two huge flags, representing the fallen twin towers, through the streets of New York City.

The Legacy of September 11

An event as momentous as the attack on September 11 lives on in many ways. The families and close friends of the victims and the survivors were profoundly changed. The government put in place many new policies to confront the threat of terrorism. It created the new Department of Homeland Security to coordinate all efforts to stop terrorism. New rules about immigration were written, affecting the lives of many. Tighter security rules affected every American who traveled by airplane or train. And, of course, the lives of many soldiers and sailors—and their families—were changed by war.

Perhaps the biggest change, however, was that Americans felt vulnerable as never before. The September 11 attack was not the first time terrorists had struck on American soil, but it was the most devastating. With simple and evil cunning, terrorists had killed far more people than ever before and destroyed two of the world's tallest buildings. After September 11, Americans realized that in spite of their nation's immense wealth and power, the threat of terrorism is always present.

Future Attack
"There will be another terrorist attack. We will not be able to stop it. It's something we all live with."

FBI Director Robert Mueller, 2002

43

Time Line

1979	November 4: Americans are taken hostage in Iran.
1983	April 18: Terrorist attack at U.S. embassy in Beirut, Lebanon.
	October 23: Terrorist attack on Marine barracks in Beirut.
1985	June 14: Terrorists hijack an airliner, killing one American hostage.
	October 7-10: Terrorists hijack cruise ship, killing one American hostage.
1988	December 21: Terrorist attack brings down Pan Am Flight 103.
1990	August 2: Iraq invades Kuwait.
1991	January 16–February 27: Gulf War.
1993	February 26: First attack on World Trade Center kills six people.
1998	August 7: Al Qaeda attacks U.S. embassies in Nairobi, Kenya, and Dar-es-Salaam, Tanzania.
	August 20: United States attacks al Qaeda camps in Afghanistan.
1999	December 14: Al Qaeda agent Ahmed Ressam is arrested in Washington.
2000	October 12: Al Qaeda attack on USS *Cole* in Yemen kills seventeen sailors.
2001	September 11: 8:15 A.M.: American Flight 11 is hijacked.
	By 8:45 A.M.: United Flight 175 is in control of hijackers.
	8:48 A.M.: American Flight 11 hits north tower of World Trade Center.
	By 9:00 A.M.: American Flight 77 is in control of hijackers.
	9:03 A.M.: United Flight 175 hits south tower of World Trade Center.
	By 9:37 A.M.: United Flight 93 is in control of hijackers.
	9:37 A.M.: American Flight 77 hits Pentagon.
	9:59 A.M.: South tower collapses.
	10:10 A.M.: United Flight 93 crashes near Shanksville, Pennsylvania.
	10:28 A.M.: North tower collapses.
	September 14: Memorial services are held for those who died on September 11.
	October 7: U.S. and British forces begin attacking Taliban and al Qaeda sites in Afghanistan.
	December: Taliban government collapses and temporary government is established in Afghanistan.
2002	U.S. government establishes Department of Homeland Security.
	December: United Nations inspectors enter Iraq to look for evidence of weapons of mass destruction.
2003	March 21: British and U.S. troops enter Iraq and conflict begins.
	April: U.S. troops enter Baghdad and overthrow Iraqi government.

Glossary

alliance: agreement between groups or countries to support and defend each other.

chemical weapon: weapon that uses harmful chemicals to kill large numbers of people.

civilian: person who is not a member of the armed forces.

cruise missile: computer-guided missile that can fly long distances at high speeds and hit its targets with precision.

democratic: having to do with a democracy, which is a nation where citizens can vote on decisions about how they are governed or elect representatives to vote for them.

dictator: leader who has complete power within a country.

economy: system of producing and distributing goods and services.

extremist: person who takes such a radical view of an issue that he or she will take dangerous or violent actions.

hijack: take control, illegally and by force, of an airplane or other vehicle.

hostage: person captured and held by someone who threatens to harm the person unless his or her demands are met.

martyr: person who dies for a cause he or she believes in.

Middle East: region of the world from Israel in the west to Iran in the east.

moderate: capable of forming opinions that are not extreme and that try to include more than one viewpoint.

patriotism: feeling and expression of loyalty to one's own country above all others.

radical: wanting to make extreme changes in society.

refugee: person forced by war, cruelty, or intolerance to move from his or her home and live somewhere else.

sanctions: restrictions placed by a group of nations on a nation that is not abiding by international law in order to punish that nation or persuade it to change.

socialist: person who believes that governments should control important parts of the economy and make many decisions about people's lives.

terrorist: person who performs acts of violence in order to make a political point or force a change in government policy.

United Nations: organization formed after World War II and now made up of nearly two hundred nations. It has the power to pass international laws, enforce peace between nations, and decide on issues that affect the whole world.

Further Information

Books

Foster, Leila Merrell. *The Story of the Persian Gulf War* (Cornerstones of Freedom). Children's Press, 1991.

Frank, Mitch. *Understanding September 11th: Answering Questions about the Attacks on America.* Viking, 2002.

Gard, Carolyn. *The Attacks on the World Trade Center: February 26, 1993 and September 11, 2001* (Terrorist Attacks). Rosen, 2003.

Landau, Elaine. *Osama bin Laden: A War Against the West.* Twenty-First Century Books, 2002.

Longman, Jere. *Among the Heroes: United Flight 93 and the Passengers and Crew Who Fought Back.* Harper Collins, 2002.

Skinner, Peter. *World Trade Center.* Metro, 2002.

Taylor, Robert and Stephen Currie. *The History of Terrorism* (Terrorism Library). Lucent, 2002.

Web Sites

www.911digitalarchive.org A collection of information about the September 11 attacks, including primary sources such as audio and video clips and documents.

news.bbc.co.uk/1/hi/in_depth/world/2001/war_on_terror British Broadcasting Corporation's news site has information on the war against terrorism and background stories on the people and events.

www.cnn.com/SPECIALS/2001/trade.center/index.html News network CNN has many stories on the September 11 attacks, al Qaeda, the war in Afghanistan, and similar topics.

www.un.org/Pubs/CyberSchoolBus United Nations' youth web site offers a global perspective on important world issues and information about the UN's work.

Index

Page numbers in *italics* indicate maps and diagrams. Page numbers in **bold** indicate other illustrations.